# Away In A Manger

## A Crocheted Nativity

by Cindy Harris



# Table Of Contents



Leisure Arts Inc • Maumelle Arkansas

# GENERAL INSTRUCTIONS

## ABBREVIATIONS

BLO Back Loop(s) Only
ch(s) chain(s)
dc double crochet(s)
FLO Front Loop(s) Only
hdc half double crochet(s)
mm millimeters
Rnd(s) Round(s)
sc single crochet(s)
st(s) stitch(es)
YO yarn over

★ — work instructions following ★ as many **more** times as indicated in addition to the first time.

( ) — work enclosed instructions **as many** times as specified by the number immediately following or contains explanatory remarks.

## MARKERS

Markers are used to help distinguish the beginning of each round being worked. Place a 2" scrap piece of yarn before the first stitch of each round, moving marker after each round is complete.

## CHANGING COLORS

Work the last stitch to within one step of completion, hook new yarn ***(Fig. 1)*** and draw through loops on hook. Cut old yarn and work over both ends, unless otherwise instructed.

**Fig.1**

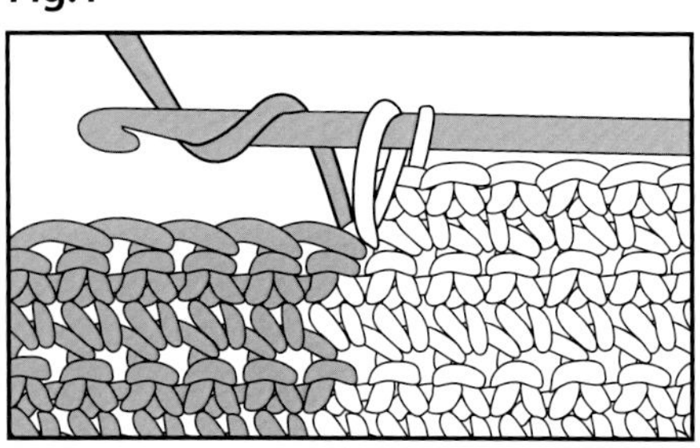

## BACK OR FRONT LOOP ONLY

Work only in loop(s) indicated by arrow ***(Fig. 2)***.

**Fig. 2**

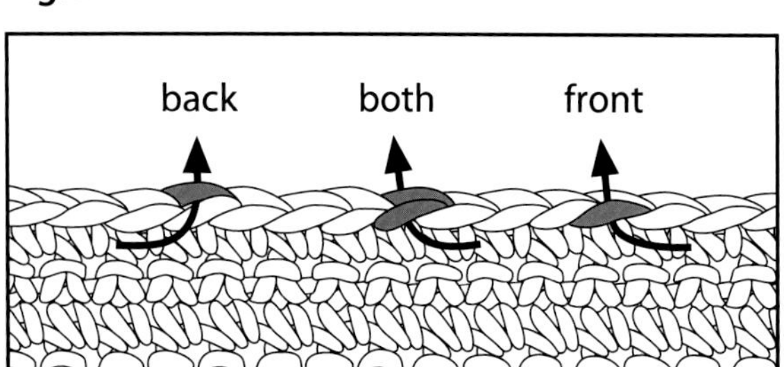


## FREE LOOPS

When instructed to work in free loops of a beginning chain, work in loop indicated by arrow **(Fig. 3a)**.

After working in Back Loops Only on a round, there will be a ridge of unused loops. These are called the free loops. Later, when instructed to work in the free loops of the same round, work in these loops ***(Fig. 3b)***.

**Fig. 3a**

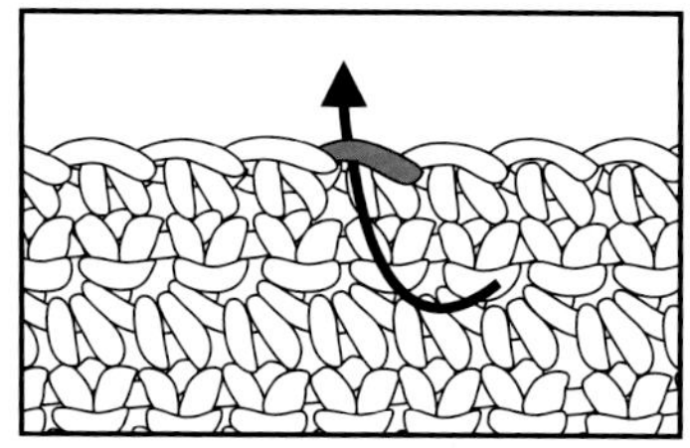

**Fig. 3b**

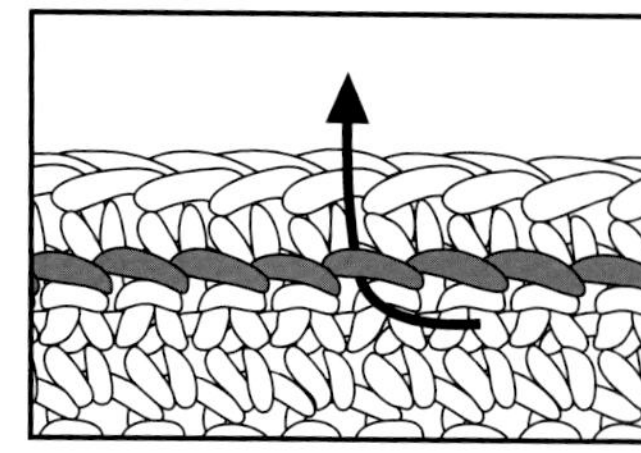

## LONG SC

Sc in sc one row or round **below** next sc ***(Fig. 4)***, skip sc behind long sc.

**Fig. 4**

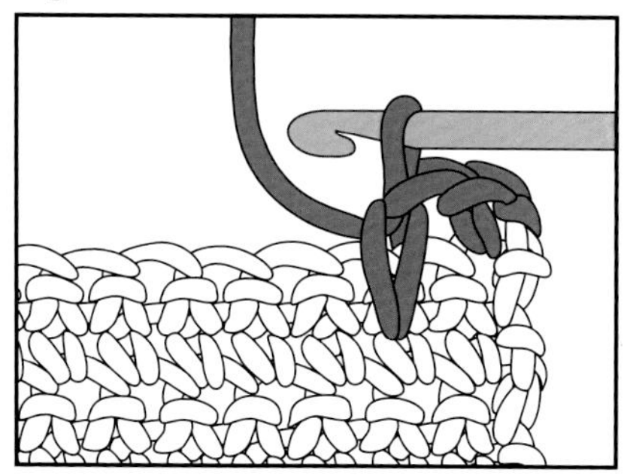

## REVERSE SINGLE CROCHET

Working from **left to right**, ★ insert hook in stitch to right of hook ***(Fig. 5a)***, YO and draw through, under and to left of loop on hook (2 loops on hook) ***(Fig. 5b)***, YO and draw through both loops on hook ***(Fig. 5c)*** **(reverse sc made, *Fig. 5d*)**; repeat from ★ around.

**Fig. 5a**

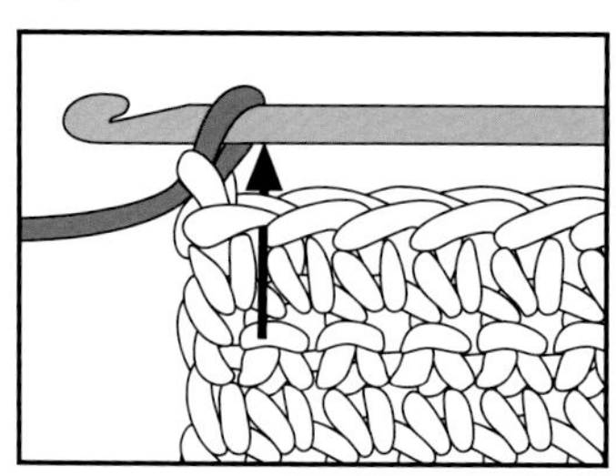

**Fig. 5b**

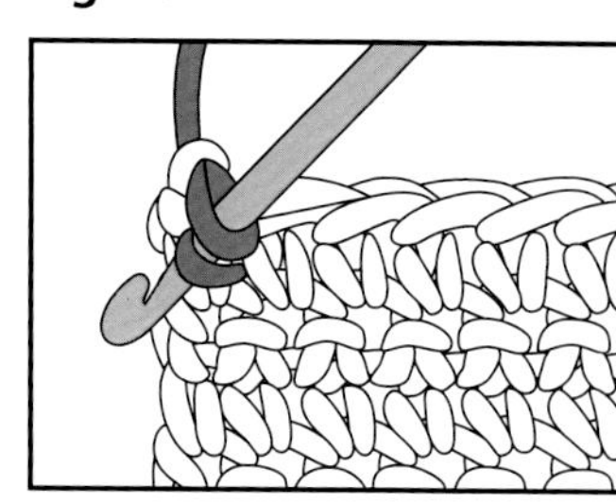

**Fig. 5c**

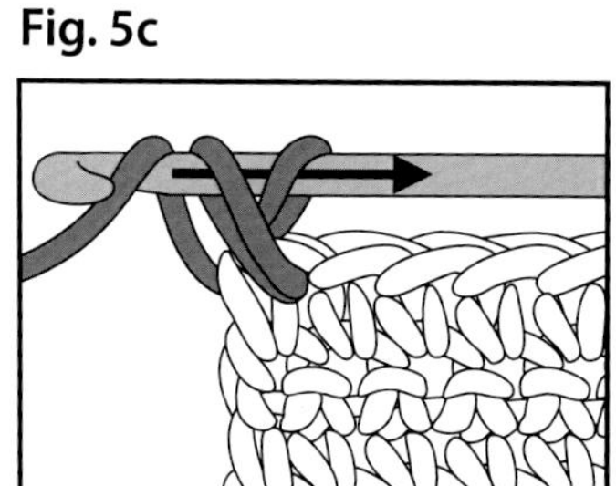

**Fig. 5d**

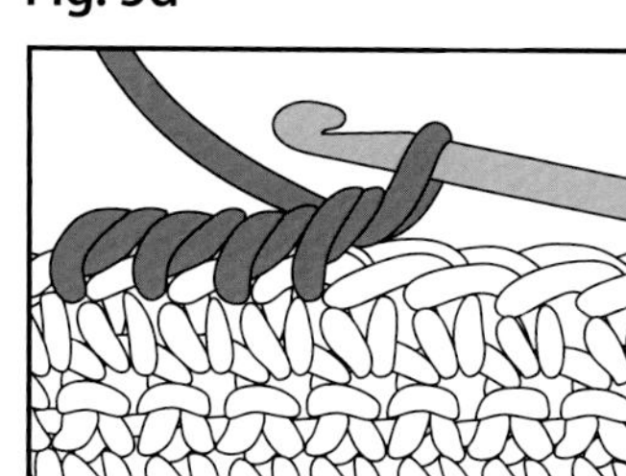

### STRAIGHT STITCH

Straight Stitch is just what the name implies, a single, straight stitch. Come up at 1 and go down at 2 ***(Fig. 6)***.

**Fig. 6**

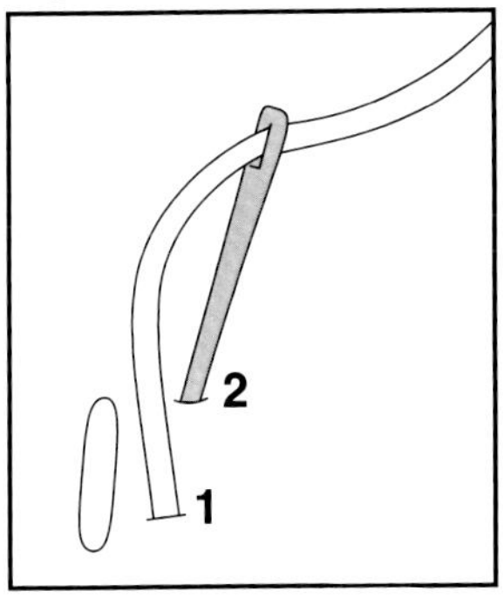


### OUTLINE STITCH

Come up at 1, holding yarn above needle, insert needle down at 2 and up again at 3 (halfway between 1 and 2) ***(Fig. 7a)***; pull through. Insert needle down at 4 and up again at 2, making sure yarn is above needle ***(Fig. 7b)***; pull through. Continue in this manner.

**Fig. 7a**

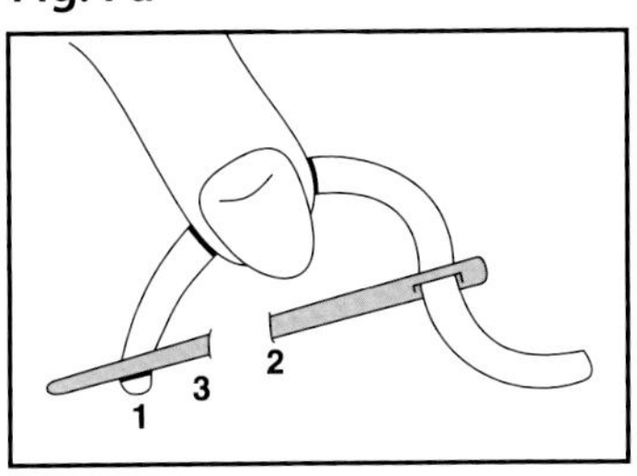


**Fig. 7b**

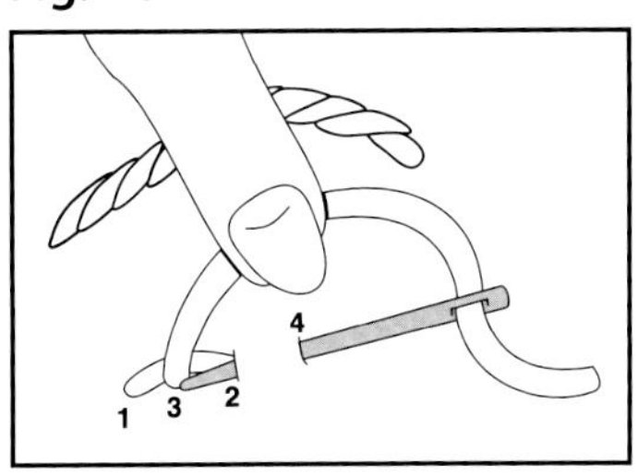


### SATIN STITCH

Come up at odd numbers and go down at even numbers, with stitches touching but not overlapping ***(Fig. 8)***.
Take care to keep edges even.

**Fig. 8**

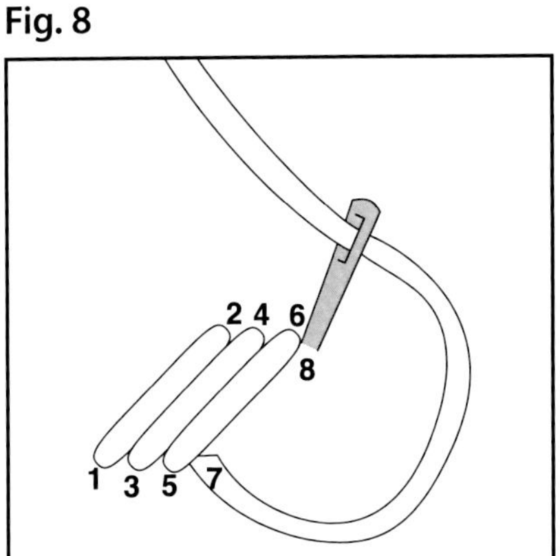


### FRINGE

Cut a piece of cardboard 3" square.

Wind the yarn **loosely** and **evenly** around the cardboard until the card is filled, then cut across one end; repeat as needed.

Hold two strands together and fold in half.

With **wrong** side of piece facing and using a crochet hook, draw the folded end up through a row and pull all strands through the folded end ***(Fig. 9a)***: draw the knot up **tightly** ***(Fig. 9b)***.

Lay flat on a hard surface and trim the ends.

**Fig. 9a**

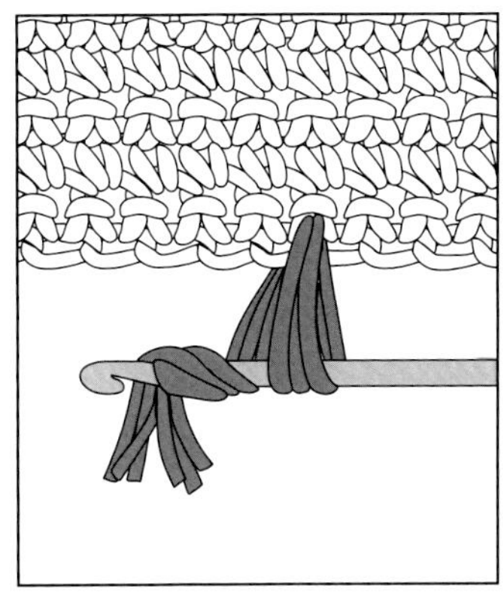

**Fig. 9b**

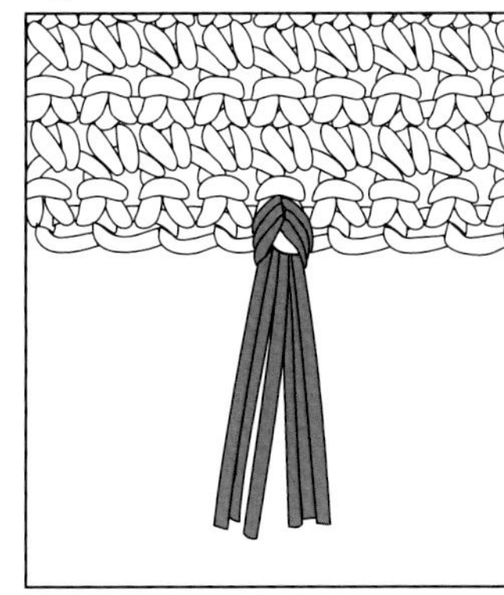

**Metallic Heavy Braid used in photography courtesy of:**
**Kreinik Mfg. Co., Inc.**
**9199 Reisterstown Rd., Ste 209B**
**Owings Mills, MD 21117**

# INSTRUCTIONS

## BASIC BASE

**Rnd 1** (Right side)**:** Ch 2, 6 sc in second ch from hook; do **not** join, place marker ***(see Markers, page 2)***: 6 sc.

***Note:*** Loop a short piece of yarn around any stitch to mark last round as **right** side.

**Rnd 2**: 2 Sc in each sc around: 12 sc.

**Rnd 3:** (Sc in next sc, 2 sc in next sc) around: 18 sc.

**Rnd 4:** (Sc in next 2 sc, 2 sc in next sc) around: 24 sc.

**Rnd 5:** (Sc in next 3 sc, 2 sc in next sc) around, slip st in next sc; finish off: 30 sc.

*Continued on page 4.*

## BASIC BODY

**Rnd 1** (Right side): Ch 2, 6 sc in second ch from hook; do **not** join, place marker: 6 sc.

**Note:** Mark last round as **right** side.

**Rnd 2**: 2 Sc in each sc around: 12 sc.

**Rnd 3:** (Sc in next sc, 2 sc in next sc) around: 18 sc.

**Rnds 4-8:** Sc in each sc around.

To **decrease** (uses next 2 sc), pull up a loop in next 2 sc, YO and draw through all 3 loops on hook.

**Rnd 9:** (Sc in next sc, decrease) around: 12 sc.

**Rnd 10:** Sc in each sc around, slip st in next sc changing to color indicated ***(Fig. 1, page 2)***; stuff firmly (Head), remove marker.

**Rnd 11:** Ch 1, sc in each sc around; join with slip st to first sc.

**Rnd 12:** Ch 1, sc in same st and in next 2 sc, 2 sc in next sc, (sc in next 3 sc, 2 sc in next sc) around; join with slip st to first sc: 15 sc.

**Rnds 13 and 14:** Ch 1, sc in each sc around; join with slip st to first sc.

**Rnd 15:** Ch 1, sc in same st and in next 3 sc, 2 sc in next sc, (sc in next 4 sc, 2 sc in next sc) around; join with slip st to first sc: 18 sc.

**Rnds 16 and 17:** Ch 1, sc in each sc around; join with slip st to first sc.

**Rnd 18:** Ch 1, sc in same st and in next 4 sc, 2 sc in next sc, (sc in next 5 sc, 2 sc in next sc) around: join with slip st to first sc: 21 sc.

**Rnds 19 and 20:** Ch 1, sc in each sc around; join with slip st to first sc.

**Rnd 21:** Ch 1, sc in same st and in next 5 sc, 2 sc in next sc, (sc in next 6 sc, 2 sc in next sc) around; join with slip st to first sc: 24 sc.

**Rnds 22 and 23:** Ch 1, sc in each sc around; join with slip st to first sc.

**Rnd 24:** Ch 1, sc in same st and in next 6 sc, 2 sc in next sc, (sc in next 7 sc, 2 sc in next sc) around; join with slip st to first sc: 27 sc.

**Rnds 25 and 26:** Ch 1, sc in each sc around; join with slip st to first sc.

**Rnd 27:** Ch 1, sc in same st and in next 7 sc, 2 sc in next sc, (sc in next 8 sc, 2 sc in next sc) around; join with slip st to first sc: 30 sc

Place plastic foam cone inside Body.

**Rnd 28:** Ch 1, with **wrong** side of Base against bottom of cone, Head toward you, and working in sc on Rnd 27 of Body **and** Rnd 5 of Base, sc in same st and in next 3 sc, 2 sc in next sc, (sc in next 4 sc, 2 sc in next sc) around; join with slip st to first sc, finish off.

## BASIC ARM (Make 2)

**Rnd 1** (Right side): Ch 2, 6 sc in second ch from hook; join with slip st to first sc: 6 sc.

**Note:** Mark last round as **right** side.

**Rnds 2-4:** Ch 1, sc in each sc around; join with slip st to first sc.

**Rnd 5:** Ch 1, sc in same st, 2 sc in next sc, (sc in next sc, 2 sc in next sc) around; join with slip st to first sc: 9 sc.

**Rnds 6 and 7:** Ch 1, sc in each sc around; join with slip st to first sc.

**Rnd 8:** Ch 1, sc in same st and in next sc, 2 sc in next sc, (sc in next 2 sc, 2 sc in next sc) around; join with slip st to first sc: 12 sc.

**Rnd 9:** Ch 1, sc in each sc around; join with slip st to first sc, finish off.

## BASIC HAND

With **right** side of Arm facing, join yarn with slip st in BLO of any sc on Rnd 9 ***(Fig. 2, page 2)***; ch 3, 4 dc in same st, drop loop from hook, insert hook in top of beginning ch-3, hook dropped loop and draw through, ch 1 to close; finish off.

# FACIAL FEATURES

Use Cover Photo as a guide for placement of all facial features.

**Nose:** With yarn and working Straight Stitch ***(Fig. 6, page 3)***, make 4 vertical stitches in center front of Head.

**Closed eyes:** With 6 strands of embroidery floss and working Outline Stitch ***(Figs. 7a & b, page 3)***, add eyes approximately ¼" long just above and on each side of nose.

**Open eyes:** With 6 strands of lighter colored embroidery floss and working Straight Stitch, work 3 or 4 horizontal stitches approximately $\frac{5}{16}$" long just above and on each side of nose. Then, with darker colored embroidery floss, work 3 or 4 vertical stitches around center of horizontal stitches to form pupil of eye. Do **not** pull too tight.

**Eyebrows:** With six strands of embroidery floss and working Outline Stitch ***(Figs, 7a & b, page 3)***, add eyebrow above each eye.

**Mouth:** With 6 strands of embroidery floss and working Outline Stitch, add mouth.

**Beard:** With a double strand of yarn and beginning at side of face, work Satin Stitch ***(Fig. 8, page 3)*** vertically across lower part of face. For a longer beard, work longer stitches extending down into Torso.

**Moustache:** With a double strand of yarn and working Satin Stitch, beginning under nose and working toward outer edge of beard, work 2 stitches on each side, leaving a small opening in the center for mouth.

# THE HOLY FAMILY

## MATERIALS

Worsted Weight Yarn, approximately:

**Mary:** Rose - 40 yards
Dark Blue - 23 yards
Light Peach - 11 yards
Dark Brown - 7 yards
Light Rose - 6 yards
Blue - small amount

**Joseph:** Green - 38 yards
Gold - 28 yards
Light Peach - 11 yards
Dark Brown - small amount

**Baby Jesus:** Light Brown - 20 yards
Light Peach - 8 yards
Dark Brown - small amount

Metallic Gold Heavy Braid, approximately 12 yards **total**
Crochet hook, size F (3.75 mm) or size needed for gauge
2 Plastic foam cones - 4" high x 2½" diameter
Polyester stuffing
Yarn needle
Tapestry needle
Embroidery floss - Black, Blue and Pink, small amount **each**

**GAUGE:** 18 sc and 16 rows = 4"

## MARY

**Finished Size:** Approximately 6½" tall

### BASE

With Rose, work same as Basic Base, page 3.

### BODY

**Rnds 1-10:** With Light Peach, work same as Basic Body, page 4, changing to Rose at end of Rnd 10: 12 sc.

**Rnds 11-28:** Work same as Basic Body.

### ARM (Make 2)

**Rnds 1-7:** With Rose, work same as Basic Arm, page 4, changing to Blue when joining at end of Rnd 7: 9 sc.

**Rnd 8:** Ch 1, sc in same st and in next sc, 2 sc in next sc, (sc in next 2 sc, 2 sc in next sc) around; join with slip st to first sc changing to Dark Blue: 12 sc.

**Rnd 9:** Ch 1, sc in each sc around; join with slip st to first sc, finish off.

### HAND

With Light Peach, work same as Basic Hand, page 4.

### MANTLE

With Dark Blue, ch 38 **loosely**.

**Row 1** (Wrong side)**:** Sc in second ch from hook and in each ch across: 37 sc.

***Note:*** Mark last row as **wrong** side.

**Rows 2-9:** Ch 1, turn; sc in each sc across, changing to Light Rose in last sc of Row 9.

### EDGING

**Rnd 1**: Ch 1, turn; 3 sc in first sc, sc in each sc across to last sc, 3 sc in last sc; working in end of rows, skip first row, sc in each row across to last row, skip last row; working in free loops of beginning ch ***(Fig. 3a, page 2)***, 3 sc in first ch, sc in each ch across to last ch, 3 sc in last ch; working in end of rows, skip first row, sc in each row across to last row, skip last row; join with slip st to first sc changing to Rose: 96 sc.

**Rnd 2:** Ch 1, do **not** turn; sc in same st, 3 sc in next sc, sc in next 37 sc, 3 sc in next sc, sc in next 9 sc, 3 sc in next sc, sc in next 37 sc, 3 sc in next sc, sc in next 8 sc; join with slip st to first sc, finish off.

With **wrong** sides of one long end together, whipstitch seam, working through both loops on each side ***(Fig. 10)***. Fold point approximately 1" down on the **right** side and secure to seam.

**Fig. 10**

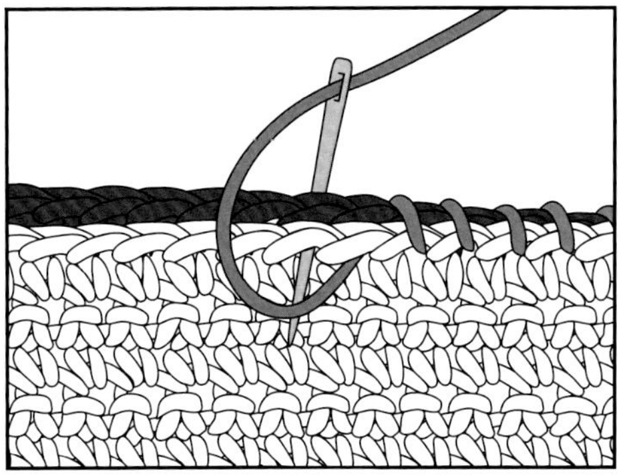

### HALO

**Foundation Rnd:** With Metallic ch 4, 11 dc in fourth ch from hook; join with slip st to top of beginning ch-4: 12 sts.

**Row 1:** Ch 3 **(counts as first dc)**, turn; 2 dc in same st, ★ ch 1, skip next dc, 3 dc in next dc; repeat from ★ 2 times **more**, leave remaining 5 dc unworked.

**Edging:** Ch 1, turn; working in each dc and in each ch, sc in first st, (ch 2, sc in next st) across; working in unworked dc of Row 1, sc in next 5 dc; join with slip st to first sc, finish off.

## FINISHING

Using Cover Photo as a guide for placement, sew Arms to Body. Tack Hands together and secure to Body.

Add Black closed eyes and Pink mouth ***(see Facial Features, page 4)***.

**Hair:** Cut 24 strands of Dark Brown, each 10" long. Place on Head with equal lengths on each side of face. Sew Hair to center of Head. Trim to desired length. Place Mantle on Head and secure with a few stitches.

Sew Halo to back of Mantle.

## JOSEPH

**Finished Size:** Approximately 6½" tall

### BASE

With Gold, work same as Basic Base, page 3.

### BODY

**Rnds 1-10:** With Light Peach, work same as Basic Body, page 4, changing to Green at end of Rnd 10: 12 sc.

***Note:*** When instructed to drop a color, carry yarn **loosely** on **wrong** side.

**Rnds 11-23:** Work same as Basic Body, changing to Gold when joining at end of Rnd 23; drop Green; 24 sc.

**Rnd 24:** Ch 1, sc in same st and in next 6 sc, 2 sc in next sc, (sc in next 7 sc, 2 sc in next sc) around, drop Gold; join with slip st to first sc changing to Green: 27 sc.

**Rnds 25 and 26:** Ch 1, sc in each sc around; join with slip st to first sc, changing to Gold when joining at end of Rnd 26; cut Green.

**Rnds 27 and 28:** Work same as Basic Body.

### ARM (Make 2)

**Rnds 1-4:** With Green, work same as Basic Arm, page 4, changing to Gold when joining at end of Rnd 4; drop Green: 6 sc.

**Rnd 5:** Ch 1, sc in same st, 2 sc in next sc, (sc in next sc, 2 sc in next sc) around, drop Gold; join with slip st to first sc changing to Green: 9 sc.

**Rnds 6 and 7:** Ch 1, sc in each sc around; join with slip st to first sc, changing to Gold when joining at end of Rnd 7; cut Green.

**Rnd 8:** Ch 1, sc in same st and in next sc, 2 sc in next sc, (sc in next 2 sc, 2 sc in next sc) around: join with slip st to first sc: 12 sc.

**Rnd 9:** Ch 1, sc in each sc around; join with slip st to first sc, finish off.

### HAND

With Light Peach, work same as Basic Hand, page 4.

### MANTLE

With Green, ch 25 **loosely**.

**Row 1** (Right side)**:** Sc in second ch from hook and in each ch across: 24 sc.

***Note:*** Mark last row as **right** side.

**Row 2:** Ch 1, turn; sc in each sc across, changing to Gold in last sc.

**Row 3:** Ch 1, turn; sc in each sc across.

**Row 4:** Ch 1, turn; sc in each sc across, changing to Green in last sc.

**Row 5:** Ch 1, turn; sc in each sc across.

**Row 6:** Ch 1, turn; sc in each sc across, changing to Gold in last sc.

**Rows 7-10:** Repeat Rows 3-6.

### FIRST FLAP

**Row 1:** Ch 1, turn; sc in first 18 sc, leave remaining 6 sc unworked: 18 sc.

**Row 2:** Ch 1, turn; sc in each sc across, changing to Green in last sc.

**Rows 3 and 4:** Ch 1, turn; sc in each sc across. Finish off.

### SECOND FLAP

**Row 1:** With **right** side facing and working in free loops of beginning ch ***(Fig. 3a, page 2)***, skip first 6 chs and join Gold with slip st in next ch; ch 1, sc in same st and in next 17 chs: 18 sc.

**Rows 2-4:** Work same as First Flap.

### TRIM

With one strand of Green and one strand of Gold held together, ch 16 (tie); with **right** side of Mantle facing, beginning at left corner and working in end of Rows 1-10, work reverse sc in each row across ***(Figs. 5a-d, page 2)***. ch 16 (tie); finish off.

### FINISHING

Using Photo as a guide for placement, sew Arms to Body. Tack hands together and secure to Body.

Add Light Peach nose, Black closed eyes and eyebrows, and Dark Brown beard and moustache ***(see Facial Features, page 4)***.

Trim yarn ends on ties. Place Mantle on Head with **right** side of Trim just above eyes; secure with a few stitches. Pull ties to back of Head and tie securely **over** Mantle. Tuck corner of flaps under ties.

## BABY JESUS

**Finished Size:** Approximately 3" tall

**Rnd 1** (Right side)**:** With Light Peach ch 2, 6 sc in second ch from hook; do **not** join, place marker **(see Markers, page 2)**: 6 sc.

***Note:*** Loop a short piece of yarn around any stitch to mark last round as **right** side.

**Rnd 2:** 2 Sc in each sc around: 12 sc.

**Rnds 3-5:** Sc in each sc around.

To **decrease** (uses next 2 sc), pull up a loop in next 2 sc, YO and draw through all 3 loops on hook.

**Rnd 6:** (Sc in next sc, decrease) around: 8 sc.

**Rnd 7:** Sc in each sc around.

**Rnd 8:** (Sc in next sc, 2 sc in next sc) around: 12 sc.

**Rnds 9-12:** Sc in each sc around. Stuff firmly.

**Rnd 13:** Decrease around: 6 sc.

**Rnd 14:** (Skip next sc, slip st in next sc) around; finish off.

## BLANKET

With Light Brown, ch 10 **loosely**.

**Row 1** (Right side)**:** Sc in second ch from hook and in each ch across: 9 sc.

**Note:** Mark last row as **right** side.

**Row 2:** Ch 1, turn; sc in each sc across.

**Row 3:** Ch 1, turn; sc in first sc, ★ work long sc ***(Fig. 4, page 2)***, sc in next sc; repeat from ★ across.

**Rows 4-6:** Ch 1, turn; sc in each sc across.

**Rows 7-22:** Repeat Rows 3-6, 4 times. Finish off.

## HOOD

**Row 1:** With **right** side facing and working in end of rows, join Light Brown with slip st in Row 22; ch 1, sc in same row and in next 12 rows, leave remaining 9 rows unworked: 13 sc.

**Row 2:** Ch 1, turn; sc in each sc across.

**Row 3:** Ch 1, turn; sc in first sc, (work long sc, sc in next sc) across.

**Rows 4-6:** Ch 1, turn; sc in each sc across.

**Row 7:** Ch 1, turn; sc in first sc, (work long sc, sc in next sc) across.

**Row 8:** Ch 1, turn; decrease across to last sc, sc in last sc, slip st in first st of Row 8 to form Hood; finish off.

## HALO

**Foundation Rnd:** With Metallic ch 2, 12 sc in second ch from hook; join with slip st to first sc: 12 sc.

**Row 1:** Ch 3 **(counts as first dc)**, turn; 2 dc in same st, ★ ch 1, skip next sc, 3 dc in next sc; repeat from ★ once **more**, leave remaining 7 sc unworked: 9 dc.

**Edging:** Ch 1, turn; working in each dc and in each ch, sc in first st, (ch 2, sc in next st) across; working in unworked sc of Row 1, sc in next 7 sc; join with slip st to first sc, finish off.

## FINISHING

Using Cover Photo as a guide for placement, add Light Peach nose, Blue closed eyes, and Pink mouth ***(see Facial Features, page 4)***.

With Dark Brown and working Straight Stitch, add Hair.

Place Baby Jesus in Blanket, overlap side and sew in place.

Sew Halo to back of Hood.

# ANGEL

**Finished Size:** Approximately 6½" tall

## MATERIALS

Worsted Weight Yarn, approximately:
White - 60 yards
Light Peach - 11 yards
Yellow - 9 yards
Metallic Gold Heavy Braid, approximately 12 yards
Crochet hook, size F (3.75 mm) or size needed for gauge
Plastic foam cone - 4" high x 2½" diameter
Polyester stuffing
Yarn needle
Tapestry needle
Embroidery floss - Black and Pink, small amount **each**

**GAUGE:** 18 sc and 16 rows = 4"

## BASE

With White, work same as Basic Base, page 3.

## BODY

**Rnds 1-10:** With Light Peach, work same as Basic Body, page 4, changing to White at end of Rnd 10:12 sc.

**Rnd 11:** Ch 1, sc in each sc around; join with slip st to BLO of first sc ***(Fig. 2, page 2)***.

**Rnd 12:** Ch 1, working in BLO, sc in same st and in next 2 sc, 2 sc in next sc, (sc in next 3 sc, 2 sc in next sc) around; join with slip st to both loops of first sc: 15 sc.

**Rnds 13 and 14:** Ch 1, working in both loops, sc in each sc around; join with slip st to first sc.

**Rnd 15:** Ch 1, sc in same st and in next 3 sc, 2 sc in next sc, (sc in next 4 sc, 2 sc in next sc) around; join with slip st to first sc: 18 sc.

**Rnds 16 and 17:** Ch 1, sc in each sc around; join with slip st to first sc.

**Rnd 18:** Ch 1, sc in same st and in next 4 sc, 2 sc in next sc, (sc in next 5 sc, 2 sc in next sc) around; join with slip st to first sc: 21 sc.

**Rnds 19 and 20:** Ch 1, sc in each sc around; join with slip st to first sc.

**Rnd 21:** Ch 1, sc in same st and in next 5 sc, 2 sc in next sc, (sc in next 6 sc, 2 sc in next sc) around; join with slip st to first sc: 24 sc.

**Rnds 22:** Ch 1, sc in each sc around; join with slip st to first sc.

**Rnds 23:** Ch 1, sc in each sc around; join with slip st to BLO of first sc.

**Rnd 24:** Ch 1, working in BLO, sc in same st and in next 6 sc, 2 sc in next sc, (sc in next 7 sc, 2 sc in next sc) around; join with slip st to both loops of first sc: 27 sc.

**Rnd 25:** Ch 1, working in both loops, sc in each sc around; join with slip st to BLO of first sc.

**Rnd 26:** Ch 1, working in BLO, sc in each sc around; join with slip st to both loops of first sc.

**Rnd 27:** Ch 1, working in both loops, sc in same st and in next 7 sc, 2 sc in next sc, (sc in next 8 sc, 2 sc in next sc) around; join with slip st to BLO of first sc: 30 sc.

Place plastic foam cone inside Body.

**Rnd 28:** Ch 1, with **wrong** side of Base against bottom of cone, Head toward you, and working in BLO of sc on Rnd 27 of Body **and** both loops of sc on Rnd 5 of Base, sc in same st and in next 3 sc, 2 sc in next sc, (sc in next 4 sc, 2 sc in next sc) around; join with slip st to first sc, finish off.

**Neck Ruffle:** With Head toward you and working in free loops on Rnd 11 ***(Fig. 3b, page 2)***, join White with slip st in any sc; ch 1, sc in same st, ch 2, (sc in next sc, ch 2) around; join with slip st to first sc, finish off.

## SKIRT RUFFLES

**Top:** With Head toward you and working in free loops on Rnd 23, join White with slip st in any sc; ch 1, sc in same st, ch 2, (sc in next sc, ch 2) around; join with slip st to first sc, finish off.

**Center:** With Head toward you and working in free loops on Rnd 25, join White with slip st in any sc; ch 1, sc in same st, ch 2, (sc in next sc, ch 2) around; join with slip st to first sc, finish off.

**Bottom:** With Head toward you and working in free loops on Rnd 27, join White with slip st in any sc; ch 1, sc in same st, ch 2, (sc in next sc, ch 2) around; join with slip st to first sc, finish off.

## ARM (Make 2)

**Rnds 1-7:** With White, work same as Basic Arm, page 4: 9 sc.

**Rnd 8:** Ch 1, sc in same st and in next sc, 2 sc in next sc, (sc in next 2 sc, 2 sc in next sc) around; join with slip st to BLO of first sc: 12 sc.

**Rnd 9:** Ch 1, working in BLO, sc in each sc around; join with slip st to both loops of first sc, finish off.

**First Ruffle:** With **right** side facing, Rnd 1 toward you, and working in free loops on Rnd 8, join White with slip st in any sc; ch 1, sc in same st, ch 2, (sc in next sc, ch 2) around; join with slip st to first sc, finish off.

**Second Ruffle:** With **right** side facing, Rnd 1 toward you, and working in FLO on Rnd 9, join White with slip st in any sc; ch 1, sc in same st, ch 2, (sc in next sc, ch 2) around; join with slip st to first sc, finish off.

### HAND

With Light Peach, work same as Basic Hand, page 4.

## WING (Make 2)

**Row 1:** With White ch 4, 4 dc in fourth ch from hook: 5 sts.

**Row 2:** (Right side): Ch 1, turn; 2 sc in each st across: 10 sc.

***Note:*** Mark last row as **right** side.

**Row 3:** Ch 3 **(counts as first dc, now and throughout)**, turn; dc in same st, ★ ch 1, skip next 2 sc, 2 dc in next sc; repeat from ★ across: 8dc.

**Row 4:** Ch 1, turn; sc in each dc and in each ch across: 11 sc.

**Row 5:** Ch 3, turn; dc in same st and in next sc, ch 1, skip next sc, ★ dc in next 2 sc, ch 1, skip next sc; repeat from ★ once **more**, dc in next sc, 2 dc in last sc, changing to Metallic in last sc: 10 dc.

**Row 6:** Ch 1, turn; working in each dc and in each ch, sc in first st, (ch 2, sc in next st) across: finish off.

## HALO

Work same as Mary's Halo, page 5.

## FINISHING

Using Cover Photo as a guide for placement, sew Arms to Body. Tack Hands together and secure to Body.

Sew Wings to Body.

Add Black closed eyes and Pink mouth ***(see Facial Features, page 4)***.

**Hair:** Cut 24 strands of Yellow, each 12" long. Place on Head with equal lengths on each side of face. Sew Hair to center of Head.

Trim to desired length.

Sew Halo to back of Head.

# THE WISEMEN

## MATERIALS

Worsted Weight Yarn, approximately:
- **Melchior:** Turquoise - 59 yards
  - Light Peach - 11 yards
  - Medium Brown - small amount
- **Caspar:** Blue - 69 yards
  - Brown - 11 yards
  - Black - small amount
- **Balthazar:** Red - 56 yards
  - Light Peach - 11 yards
  - Medium Brown - small amount

Metallic Gold Heavy Braid, approximately 43 yards **total**
Crochet hook, size F (3.75 mm) or size needed for gauge
3 Plastic foam cones 4" high x 2½" diameter
Polyester stuffing
Yarn needle
Tapestry needle
Embroidery floss - Black, Brown, and Ecru, small amount **each**
Miniature gifts - 3
Craft glue or glue gun

**GAUGE:** 18 sc and 16 rows = 4"

## MELCHIOR

**Finished Size:** Approximately 6½" tall

### BASE

With Turquoise, work same as Basic Base, page 3.

### BODY

**Rnds 1-10:** With Light Peach, work same as Basic Body, page 4, changing to Turquoise when joining at end of Rnd 10: 12 sc.

***Note:*** When instructed to drop a color, carry yarn **loosely** on **wrong** side.

**Rnds 11-21:** Work same as Basic Body, changing to Metallic when joining at end of Rnd 21; drop Turquoise: 24 sc.

**Rnd 22:** Ch 1, sc in each sc around, drop Metallic; join with slip st to first sc changing to Turquoise.

**Rnd 23:** Ch 1, sc in same st, work long sc ***(Fig. 4, page 2)***, (sc in next sc, work long sc) around; join with slip st to first sc.

**Rnd 24:** Ch 1, sc in same st and in next 6 sc, 2 sc in next sc, (sc in next 7 sc, 2 sc in next sc) around, drop Turquoise; join with slip st to first sc changing to Metallic: 27 sc.

**Rnd 25:** Ch 1, sc in each sc around, cut Metallic; join with slip st to first sc changing to Turquoise.

**Rnd 26:** Ch 1, sc in same st, (work long sc, sc in next sc) around; join with slip st to first sc.

**Rnds 27 and 28:** Work same as Basic Body.

*Continue on page 12.*

One
Balthazar
Casper
Three
Two
Melchior

## ARM (Make 2)

**Rnds 1-7:** With Turquoise, work same as Basic Arm, page 4, changing to Metallic when joining at end of Rnd 7; drop Turquoise: 9 sc.

**Rnd 8:** Ch 1, sc in same st and in next sc, 2 sc in next sc, (sc in next 2 sc, 2 sc in next sc) around, cut Metallic; join with slip st to first sc changing to Turquoise: 12 sc.

**Rnd 9:** Ch 1, sc in each sc around; join with slip st to first sc, finish off.

## HAND

With Light Peach, work same as Basic Hand, page 4.

## MANTLE

**Rnd 1** (Right side)**:** With Turquoise ch 2, 6 sc in second ch from hook; join with slip st to first sc: 6 sc.

***Note:*** Mark last round as **right** side.

**Rnd 2:** Ch 1, 2 sc in each sc around; join with slip st to first sc: 12 sc.

**Rnd 3:** Ch 1, sc in same st, 2 sc in next sc, (sc in next sc, 2 sc in next sc) around; join with slip st to first sc: 18 sc.

**Rnd 4:** Ch 1, sc in same st and in next sc, 2 sc in next sc, (sc in next 2 sc, 2 sc in next sc) around, drop Turquoise; join with slip st to first sc changing to Metallic: 24 sc.

**Rnd 5:** Ch 1, sc in each sc around, cut Metallic; join with slip st to first sc changing to Turquoise.

**Rnd 6:** Ch 1, sc in same st, work long sc, (sc in next sc, work long sc) around; join with slip st to first sc.

***Note:*** Begin working in rows.

**Row 1:** Ch 1, sc in same st and in next 13 sc, leave remaining 10 sc unworked: 14 sc.

**Rows 2-22:** Ch 1, turn; sc in each sc across. Finish off.

## FINISHING

Using Cover Photo as a guide for placement, sew Arms to Body.

Add Light Peach nose, Ecru and Black open eyes, and Brown eyebrows, beard, and moustache ***(see Facial Features, page 4)***.

Place Mantle on Head and secure with a few stitches.

Glue miniature gift to Hands.

# CASPAR

**Finished Size:** Approximately 7" tall

## BASE

With Blue, work same as Basic Base, page 3.

## BODY

**Rnds 1-10:** With Brown, work same as Basic Body, page 4, changing to Blue at end of Rnd 10: 12 sc.

***Note:*** When instructed to drop a color, carry yarn **loosely** on **wrong** side.

**Rnds 11-21:** Work same as Basic Body, changing to Metallic when joining at end of Rnd 21; drop Blue: 24 sc.

**Rnd 22:** Ch 1, sc in same st, work long sc ***(Fig. 4, page 2)***, (sc in next sc, work long sc) around, drop Metallic; join with slip st to first sc changing to Blue.

**Rnd 23:** Ch 1, sc in each sc around, drop Blue; join with slip st to first sc changing to Metallic.

**Rnd 24:** Ch 1, ★work long sc, (sc in next sc, work long sc) 3 times, 2 sc in next sc; repeat from ★ around, drop Metallic; join with slip st to first sc changing to Blue: 27 sc.

**Rnd 25:** Ch 1, sc in each sc around, drop Blue; join with slip st to first sc changing to Metallic.

**Rnd 26:** Ch 1, sc in same st, (work long sc, sc in next sc) around, cut Metallic; join with slip st to first sc changing to Blue.

**Rnds 27 and 28:** Work same as Basic Body.

## ARM (Make 2)

**Rnds 1-6:** With Blue, work same as Basic Arm, page 4, changing to Metallic when joining at end of Rnd 6; drop Blue: 9 sc.

**Rnd 7:** Ch 1, sc in same st, (work long sc, sc in next sc) around, cut Metallic; join with slip st to first sc changing to Blue.

**Rnds 8 and 9:** Work same as Basic Arm.

## HAND

With Brown, work same as Basic Hand, page 4.

## MANTLE

**Rnds 1-3:** With Blue, work same as Melchior's Mantle, page 12: 18 sc.

**Rnd 4:** Ch 1, sc in same st and in next sc, 2 sc in next sc, (sc in next 2 sc, 2 sc in next sc) around, drop Blue; join with slip st to first sc changing to Metallic: 24 sc.

**Rnd 5:** Ch 1, sc in same st, work long sc, (sc in next sc, work long sc) around, cut Metallic; join with slip st to first sc changing to Blue.

**Rnd 6:** Ch 1, sc in each sc around; join with slip st to first sc.

***Note:*** Begin working in rows.

**Row 1:** Ch 1, sc in same st and in next 13 sc, leave remaining 10 sc unworked: 14 sc.

**Rows 2-13:** Ch 1, turn; sc in each sc across. Finish off.

## TOP KNOT

**Rnd 1** (Right side)**:** With Blue ch 2, 6 sc in second ch from hook; join with slip st to first sc: 6 sc.

***Note:*** Mark last round as **right** side.

**Rnd 2:** Ch 1, 2 sc in each sc around, drop Blue; join with slip st to first sc changing to Metallic: 12 sc.

**Rnd 3:** Ch 1, sc in same st, work long sc, (sc in next sc, work long sc) around, cut Metallic; join with slip st to first sc changing to Blue.

**Rnd 4:** Ch 1, sc in each sc around; join with slip st to first sc, finish off.

Stuff lightly and sew Top Knot to top of Mantle, gathering tightly to shape.

## CLOAK

With Blue, ch 18 **loosely**.

**Row 1** (Right side)**:** Sc in second ch from hook and in each ch across: 17 sc.

***Note:*** Mark last row as **right** side.

**Row 2:** Ch 1, turn; 2 sc in first sc, sc in each sc across to last sc, 2 sc in last sc: 19 sc.

**Rows 3 and 4:** Ch 1, turn; sc in each sc across, changing to Metallic in last sc of Row 4.

**Row 5:** Ch 1, turn; sc in first sc, (work long sc, sc in next sc) across.

**Row 6:** Ch 1, turn; sc in each sc across, changing to Blue in last sc.

**Rows 7-10:** Ch 1, turn; sc in each sc across, changing to Metallic in last sc of Row 10.

**Row 11:** Ch 1, turn; sc in first sc, (work long sc, sc in next sc) across.

**Row 12:** Ch 1, turn; sc in each sc across, changing to Blue in last sc.

**Rows 13-16:** Ch 1, turn; sc in each sc across, changing to Metallic in last sc of Row 16.

**Rows 17 and 18:** Repeat Rows 11 and 12.

**Row 19:** Ch 1, turn; sc in each sc across, finish off.

**Ties:** With Blue, ch 12 (tie); with **right** side of Cloak facing and working in free loops of beginning ch ***(Fig. 3a, page 2)***, slip st in each ch across, ch 12 (tie); finish off.

## FINISHING

Using Cover Photo as a guide for placement, sew Arms to Body.

Add Brown nose, Ecru and Black open eyes, and Black eyebrows, beard, and moustache ***(see Facial Features, page 4)***.

Place Mantle on Head and secure with a few stitches.

Tie Cloak around shoulders.

Glue miniature gift to Hands.

# BALTHAZAR

**Finished Size:** Approximately 6½" tall

## BASE

With Red, work same as Basic Base, page 3.

## BODY

**Rnds 1-10:** With Light Peach, work same as Basic Body, page 4, changing to Red at end of Rnd 10: 12 sc.

**Rnds 11-25:** Work same as Basic Body; 27 sc.

**Rnd 26:** Ch 1, sc in each sc around; join with slip st to BLO of first sc ***(Fig. 2, page 2)***.

**Rnd 27:** Ch 1, working in BLO, sc in same st and in next 7 sc, 2 sc in next sc, (sc in next 8 sc, 2 sc in next sc) around; join with slip st to BLO of first sc: 30 sc.

Place plastic foam cone inside Body.

**Rnd 28:** Ch 1, with **wrong** side of Base against bottom of cone, Head toward you, and working in BLO of sc on Rnd 27 of Body **and** both loops of sc on Rnd 5 of Base, sc in same st and in next 3 sc, 2 sc in next sc, (sc in next 4 sc, 2 sc in next sc) around; join with slip st to first sc, finish off.

**Top Trim:** With Head toward you and working in free loops on Rnd 26 ***(Fig. 3b, page 2)***, join Metallic with slip st in any sc; ch 1, work reverse sc in each sc around ***(Figs. 5a-d, page 2)***, join with slip st to first st, finish off.

**Center Trim:** With Head toward you and working in free loops on Rnd 27, join Red with slip st in any sc; ch 1, work reverse sc in each sc around; join with slip st to first st, finish off.

**Bottom Trim:** With Head toward you and working in FLO on Rnd 28, join Metallic with slip st in any sc; ch 1, work reverse sc in each sc around; join with slip st to first st, finish off.

## ARM (Make 2)

**Rnds 1-6:** With Red, work same as Basic Arm, page 4: 9 sc.

**Rnd 7:** Ch 1, sc in each sc around; join with slip st to BLO of first sc.

**Rnd 8:** Ch 1, working in BLO, sc in same st and in next sc, 2 sc in next sc, (sc in next 2 sc, 2 sc in next sc) around; join with slip st to BLO of first sc: 12 sc.

*Continue on page 14.*

**Rnd 9:** Ch 1, working in BLO, sc in each sc around; join with slip st to both loops of first sc, finish off.

**Top Trim:** With **right** side facing, Rnd 1 toward you, and working in free loops on Rnd 7, join Metallic with slip st in any sc, ch 1, work reverse sc in each sc around; join with slip st to first st. finish off.

**Center Trim:** With **right** side facing, Rnd 1 toward you, and working in free loops on Rnd 8, join Red with slip st in any sc; ch 1, work reverse sc in each sc around; join with slip st to first st, finish off.

**Cuff Trim:** With **right** side facing, Rnd 1 toward you, and working in FLO on Rnd 9, join Metallic with slip st in any sc; ch 1, work reverse sc in each sc around; join with slip st to first st, finish off.

## HAND

With Light Peach, work same as Basic Hand, page 4.

## MANTLE

**Rnds 1-3:** With Red, work same as Melchiors Mantle, page 12: 18 sc.

**Rnd 4:** Ch 1, sc in same st and in next sc, 2 sc in next sc, (sc in next 2 sc, 2 sc in next sc) around; join with slip st to BLO of first sc: 24 sc.

**Rnds 5 and 6:** Ch 1, working in BLO, sc in each sc around; join with slip st to BLO of first sc.

***Note:*** Begin working in rows.

**Row 1:** Ch 1, working in BLO, sc in same st and in next 13 sc, leave remaining 10 sc unworked: 14 sc.

**Rows 2-16:** Ch 1, turn; working in both loops, sc in each sc across.

Finish off.

**Top Trim:** With **right** side facing, Rnd 1 toward you, and working in free loops on Rnd 4, join Metallic with slip st in any sc; ch 1, work reverse sc in each sc around; join with slip st to first st, finish off.

**Center Trim:** With **right** side facing, Rnd 1 toward you, and working in free loops on Rnd 5, join Red with slip st in any sc; ch 1, work reverse sc in each sc around; join with slip st to first st, finish off.

**Bottom Trim:** With **right** side facing, Rnd 1 toward you, and working in free loops and in FLO of unworked sc on Rnd 6, join Metallic with slip st in any sc; ch 1, work reverse sc in each sc around; join with slip st to first st, finish off.

## FINISHING

Using Cover Photo as a guide for placement, sew Arms to Body.

Add Light Peach nose, Ecru and Black open eyes, and Brown eyebrows, beard, and moustache ***(see Facial Features, page 4)***.

Place Mantle on Head and secure with a few stitches.

Glue miniature gift to Hands.

# SHEPHERDS

## MATERIALS

Worsted Weight Yarn, approximately:
- **#1:** Light Brown - 50 yards
  - Light Peach and Orange - 11 yards **each**
  - Medium Brown - small amount
- **#2:** Dark Brown - 50 yards
  - Light Brown - 20 yards
  - Light Peach - 11 yards
  - Grey - small amount
- **#3:** Grey - 49 yards
  - Orange - 20 yards
  - Light Peach - 11 yards
  - Medium Brown - small amount

Crochet hook, size F (3.75 mm) or size needed for gauge
3 Plastic foam cones - 4" high x 2½" diameter
Polyester stuffing
Yarn needle
Tapestry needle
Embroidery floss - Black, Brown, Ecru, and Grey, small amount **each**
Chenille stems - 3

**GAUGE:** 18 sc and 16 rows = 4"

## SHEPHERD #1

**Finished Size:** Approximately 6½" tall

## BASE

With Light Brown, work same as Basic Base, page 3.

## BODY

**Rnds 1-10:** With Light Peach, work same as Basic Body, page 4, changing to Light Brown at end of Rnd 10: 12 sc.

***Note:*** When instructed to drop a color, carry yarn **loosely** on **wrong** side.

**Rnds 11-21:** Work same as Basic Body, changing to Orange when joining at end of Rnd 21; drop Light Brown: 24 sc.

**Rnd 22:** Ch 1, sc in each sc around, drop Orange; join with slip st to first sc changing to Light Brown.

**Rnd 23:** Ch 1, sc in same st and in next sc, work long sc ***(Fig. 4, page 2)***, (sc in next 2 sc, work long sc) around, drop Light Brown; join with slip st to first sc changing to Orange.

**Rnd 24:** Ch 1, sc in same st and in next 6 sc, 2 sc in next sc, (sc in next 7 sc, 2 sc in next sc) around, drop Orange; join with slip st to first sc changing to Light Brown: 27 sc.

**Rnd 25:** Ch 1, sc in same st and in next sc, work long sc, (sc in next 2 sc, work long sc) around, drop Light Brown; join with slip st to first sc changing to Orange.

**Rnd 26:** Ch 1, sc in each sc around, cut Orange; join with slip st to first sc changing to Light Brown.

**Rnd 27:** Ch 1, sc in same st and in next sc, work long sc, sc in next 2 sc, work long sc, sc in next sc, 2 sc in next sc, work long sc, ★ (sc in next 2 sc, work long sc) twice, sc in next sc, 2 sc in next sc, work long sc; repeat from ★ around; join with slip st to first sc: 30 sc.

Place plastic foam cone inside Body.

**Rnd 28:** Ch 1, with **wrong** side of Base against bottom of cone, Head toward you, and working in sc on Rnd 27 of Body **and** Rnd 5 of Base, sc in same st and in next 3 sc, 2 sc in next sc, (sc in next 4 sc, 2 sc in next sc) around; join with slip st to first sc, finish off.

## ARM (Make 2)

Rnds 1-7: With Light Brown, work same as Basic Arm, page 4, changing to Orange when joining at end of Rnd 7: 9 sc.

**Rnd 8:** Ch 1, sc in same st and in next sc, 2 sc in next sc, (sc in next 2 sc, 2 sc in next sc) around, cut Orange; join with slip st to first sc changing to Light Brown: 12 sc.

**Rnd 9:** Ch 1, sc in same st and in next sc, work long sc, (sc in next 2 sc, work long sc) around; join with slip st to first sc, finish off.

## HAND

With Light Peach, work same as Basic Hand, page 4.

## MANTLE

Work same as Joseph's Mantle, page 6, substituting Light Brown for Green, and substituting Orange for Gold.

## FINISHING

Using Cover Photo as a guide for placement, sew Arms to Body.

Add Light Peach nose, Ecru and Black open eyes, and Brown eyebrows, beard, and moustache ***(see Facial Features, page 4)***.

Trim yarn ends on ties. Place Mantle on Head with **right** side of Trim just above eyes; secure with a few stitches. Pull ties to back of Head and tie securely **over** Mantle. Tuck corner of flaps under ties.

Slide chenille stem through Hands and bend to shape into a staff.

# SHEPHERD #2

**Finished Size:** Approximately 6½" tall

## BASE

With Dark Brown, work same as Basic Base, page 3.

## BODY

**Rnds 1-10:** With Light Peach, work same as Basic Body, page 4, changing to Dark Brown at end of Rnd 10: 12 sc.

***Note:*** When instructed to drop a color, carry yarn **loosely** on **wrong** side.

**Rnds 11-24:** Work same as Basic Body, changing to Light Brown when joining at end of Rnd 24; drop Dark Brown: 27 sc.

**Rnd 25:** Ch 1, sc in each sc around, drop Light Brown; join with slip st to first sc changing to Dark Brown.

**Rnd 26:** Ch 1, sc in each sc around, drop Dark Brown; join with slip st to first sc changing to Light Brown.

**Rnd 27:** Ch 1, sc in same st and in next sc, work long sc ***(Fig. 4, page 2)***, sc in next 2 sc, work long sc, sc in next sc, 2 sc in next sc, work long sc, ★ (sc in next 2 sc, work long sc) twice, sc in next sc, 2 sc in next sc, work long sc; repeat from ★ around, cut Light Brown; join with slip st to first sc changing to Dark Brown: 30 sc.

Place plastic foam cone inside Body.

**Rnd 28:** Ch 1, with **wrong** side of Base against bottom of cone, Head toward you, and working in sc on Rnd 27 of Body **and** Rnd 5 of Base, sc in same st and in next 3 sc, 2 sc in next sc, (sc in next 4 sc, 2 sc in next sc) around; join with slip st to first sc, finish off.

## ARM (Make 2)

**Rnds 1-5:** With Dark Brown, work same as Basic Arm, page 4, changing to Light Brown when joining at end of Rnd 5: 9 sc.

**Rnd 6:** Ch 1, sc in each sc around, drop Light Brown; join with slip st to first sc changing to Dark Brown.

**Rnd 7:** Ch 1, sc in each sc around, drop Dark Brown; join with slip st to first sc changing to Light Brown.

**Rnd 8:** Ch 1, sc in same st, 2 sc in next sc, work long sc, ★ sc in next sc, 2 sc in next sc, work long sc; repeat from ★ around, cut Light Brown; join with slip st to first sc changing to Dark Brown: 12 sc.

**Rnd 9:** Ch 1, sc in each sc around; join with slip st to first sc, finish off.

## HAND

With Light Peach, work same as Basic Hand, page 4.

## MANTLE

Work same as Joseph's Mantle, page 6, substituting Dark Brown for Green, and substituting Light Brown for Gold.

## FINISHING

Using Cover Photo as a guide for placement, sew Arms to Body.

Add Light Peach nose, Ecru and Black open eyes, and Grey eyebrows, beard, and moustache ***(see Facial Features, page 4)***.

Trim yarn ends on ties. Place Mantle on Head with **right** side of Trim just above eyes; secure with a few stitches. Pull ties to back of Head and tie securely **over** Mantle. Tuck corner of flaps under ties.

Slide chenille stem through Hand and bend to shape into a staff.

# SHEPHERD #3

**Finished Size:** Approximately 6½" tall

## BASE

With Grey, work same as Basic Base, page 3.

## BODY

**Rnds 1-10:** With Light Peach, work same as Basic Body, page 4, changing to Grey at end of Rnd 10: 12 sc.

***Note:*** When instructed to drop a color, carry yarn **loosely** on **wrong** side.

*Continue on page 16.*

**Rnds 11-22:** Work same as Basic Body, changing to Orange when joining at end of Rnd 22; drop Grey: 24 sc.

**Rnd 23:** Ch 1, sc in each sc around, drop Orange; join with slip st to first sc changing to Grey.

**Rnd 24:** Ch 1, sc in same st and in next 6 sc, 2 sc in next sc, (sc in next 7 sc, 2 sc in next sc) around, drop Grey; join with slip st to first sc changing to Orange: 27 sc.

**Rnd 25:** Ch 1, sc in each sc around, drop Orange; join with slip st to first sc changing to Grey.

**Rnd 26:** Ch 1, sc in each sc around, drop Grey; join with slip st to first sc changing to Orange.

**Rnd 27:** Ch 1, sc in same st and in next 7 sc, 2 sc in next sc, (sc in next 8 sc, 2 sc in next sc) around, cut Orange; join with slip st to first sc changing to Grey: 30 sc.

Place plastic foam cone inside Body.

**Rnd 28:** Ch 1, with **wrong** side of Base against bottom of cone, Head toward you, and working in sc on Rnd 27 of Body **and** Rnd 5 of Base, sc in same st and in next 3 sc, 2 sc in next sc, (sc in next 4 sc, 2 sc in next sc) around; join with slip st to first sc, finish off.

### ARM (Make 2)

**Rnds 1-7:** With Grey, work same as Basic Arm, page 4, changing to Orange when joining at end of Rnd 7: 9 sc.

**Rnd 8:** Ch 1, sc in same st and in next sc, 2 sc in next sc, (sc in next 2 sc, 2 sc in next sc) around, cut Orange; join with slip st to first sc changing to Grey: 12 sc.

**Rnd 9:** Ch 1, sc in each sc around; join with slip st to first sc, finish off.

### HAND

With Light Peach, work same as Basic Hand, page 4.

### MANTLE

Work same as Joseph's Mantle, page 6, substituting Grey for Green, and substituting Orange for Gold.

### FINISHING

Using Cover Photo as a guide for placement, sew Arms to Body. Tack one Hand to Body.

Add Light Peach nose, Ecru and Black open eyes, and Brown eyebrows, beard, and moustache ***(see Facial Features, page 4)***

Trim yarn ends on ties. Place Mantle on Head with **right** side of Trim just above eyes; secure with a few stitches. Pull ties to back of Head and tie securely **over** Mantle. Tuck corner of flaps under ties

Slide chenille stem through crook of Arm and bend to shape into a staff.

# ANIMALS

## MATERIALS

Worsted Weight Yarn, approximately:
- **Camel:** Brown - 75 yards
  - Red, Turquoise, and Blue - small amount **each**
- **Lamb:** White - 27 yards
  - Black - 6 yards
- **Donkey:** Grey - 43 yards
  - Black - 4 yards
  - Light Brown and Dark Brown - 2 yards **each**
  - Light Peach and Dark Grey - small amount **each**

Metallic Gold Heavy Braid, small amount
Crochet hook, size F (3.75 mm) or size needed for gauge
Polyester stuffing
Yarn needle
Tapestry needle
Embroidery floss - Black, Blue, and Gold - small amount **each**

**GAUGE:** 18 sc and 16 rows = 4"

## CAMEL

**Finished Size:** Approximately 7" tall

### HEAD

***Note:*** Every few rounds, stuff lightly.

**Rnd 1** (Right side): With Brown ch 2, 6 sc in second ch from hook; do **not** join, place marker ***(see Markers, page 2)***; 6 sc

***Note:*** Loop a short piece of yarn around any stitch to mark last round as **right** side.

**Rnd 2**: (Sc in next sc, 2 sc in next sc) around: 9 sc.

**Rnd 3:** (Sc in next 2 sc, 2 sc in next sc) around: 12 sc.

**Rnd 4:** Sc in each sc around.

To **decrease** (uses next 2 sc), pull up a loop in next 2 sc, YO and draw through all 3 loops on hook.

**Rnd 5:** (Sc in next 2 sc, decrease) around: 9 sc.

**Rnd 6:** (Sc in next 2 sc, 2 sc in next sc) around: 12 sc.

**Rnd 7:** (Sc in next 3 sc, 2 sc in next sc) around: 15 sc.

**Rnds 8-10:** Sc in each sc around.

**Rnd 11:** (Sc in next 3 sc, decrease) around: 12 sc.

**Rnd 12:** Decrease around: 6 sc.

**Rnd 13:** (Skip next sc, slip st in next sc) around; finish off.

### BODY

***Note:*** Every few rounds, stuff lightly.

**Rnd 1** (Right side)**:** With Brown ch 2, 6 sc in second ch from hook; do **not** join, place marker: 6 sc.

***Note:*** Mark last round as **right** side.

**Rnd 2:** 2 Sc in each sc around: 12 sc.

**Rnd 3:** (Sc in next sc, 2 sc in next sc) around: 18 sc.

**Rnds 4-6:** Sc in each sc around.

**Rnd 7:** (Sc in next 4 sc, decrease) around: 15 sc.

**Rnds 8-10:** Sc in each sc around.

**Rnd 11:** (Sc in next 4 sc, 2 sc in next sc) around: 18 sc.

**Rnds 12-14:** Sc in each sc around.

**Rnd 15:** (Sc in next sc, decrease) around: 12 sc.

**Rnd 16:** (Sc in next 4 sc, decrease) around: 10 sc.

**Rnds 17-21:** Sc in each sc around.

**Rnds 22-24:** Slip st **loosely** in next 5 sts, hdc in next 5 sts.

**Rnds 25 and 26:** Sc in each st around; at end of Rnd 26, slip st in next sc and finish off leaving a long end for sewing.

## HUMP

**Rnd 1** (Right side)**:** With Brown ch 2, 6 sc in second ch from hook; do **not** join, place marker: 6 sc.

***Note:*** Mark last round as **right** side.

**Rnd 2:** (Sc in next sc, 2 sc in next sc) around; 9 sc.

**Rnd 3:** (Sc in next 2 sc, 2 sc in next sc) around: 12 sc.

**Rnd 4:** (Sc in next 3 sc, 2 sc in next sc) around: 15 sc.

**Rnd 5:** (Sc in next 4 sc, 2 sc in next sc) around; 18 sc.

**Rnd 6:** (Sc in next 5 sc, 2 sc in next sc) around, slip st in next sc; finish off leaving a long end for sewing.

## LEG (Make 4)

***Note:*** Every few rounds, stuff lightly.

**Rnd 1** (Right side)**:** With Brown ch 2, 6 sc in second ch from hook; do not join, place marker: 6 sc.

***Note:*** Mark last round as **right** side.

**Rnd 2:** 2 Sc in each sc around: 12 sc.

**Rnd 3:** Sc in each sc around.

**Rnd 4:** Sc in next 2 sc, decrease 4 times, sc in next 2 sc: 8 sc.

**Rnd 5:** Sc in next 2 sc, decrease twice, sc in next 2 sc: 6 sc.

**Rnds 6-12:** Sc in each sc around.

**Rnd 13:** (Sc in next sc, 2 sc in next sc) around: 9 sc.

**Rnd 14:** Sc in each sc around.

**Rnd 15:** (Sc in next sc, decrease) around: 6 sc.

**Rnds 16-19:** Sc in each sc around.

**Rnd 20:** (Sc in next sc, 2 sc in next sc) around: 9 sc.

**Rnd 21:** (Sc in next 2 sc, 2 sc in next sc) around: 12 sc.

**Rnd 22:** (Sc in next 3 sc, 2 sc in next sc) around: 15 sc.

**Rnd 23:** Sc in each sc around, slip st in next sc; finish off leaving a long end for sewing.

## TAIL

With Brown, ch 13 **loosely**; slip st in second ch from hook and in each ch across; finish off leaving a long end for sewing.

## EAR (Make 2)

With Brown, ch 3 **loosely**; sc in second ch from hook and in next ch; finish off leaving a long end for sewing.

## BLANKET

**Rnd 1** (Right side)**:** With Red ch 2, 6 sc in second ch from hook; join with slip st to first sc: 6 sc.

***Note:*** Mark last round as **right** side.

**Rnd 2**: Ch 1, 2 sc in each sc around; join with slip st to first sc: 12 sc.

**Rnd 3:** Ch 1, sc in same st and in next sc, 2 sc in next sc, (sc in next 2 sc, 2 sc in next sc) around; join with slip st to first sc: 16 sc.

**Rnd 4:** Ch 1, sc in same st and in next 2 sc, 2 sc in next sc, (sc in next 3 sc, 2 sc in next sc) around: join with slip st to first sc changing to Metallic ***(Fig. 1, page 2)***: 20 sc.

**Rnd 5:** Ch 1, sc in same st, work long sc ***(Fig. 4, page 2)***, (sc in next sc, work long sc) around; join with slip st to first sc changing to Turquoise.

**Rnd 6:** Ch 1, sc in same st and in next 3 sc, 2 sc in next sc, (sc in next 4 sc, 2 sc in next sc) around; join with slip st to first sc changing to Blue: 24 sc.

**Rnd 7:** Ch 1, sc in same st, work long sc, (sc in next sc, work long sc) around; join with slip st to first sc changing to Red.

**Rnd 8:** Ch 1, sc in each sc around; join with slip st to first sc, finish off.

Add Metallic Fringe ***(Figs. 9a & b, page 3)***.

## FINISHING

Using Cover Photo as a guide for placement and holding Body with neck tilted upward, sew Head to neck with last round of Head facing toward back of Body.

Sew Legs to Body positioning feet to face Head. Sew Ears to side of Head and Tail to back of Body. Stuff Hump lightly and sew to top of Body.

Place Blanket on Hump and sew in place.

Cut 2 strands of Brown each 2" long. Hold together and tie in a knot onto end of Tail. Trim to ½".

With Metallic, make a 12" twisted cord for Reins ***(see Twisted Cord below)***.

With Black embroidery floss and working Straight Stitch ***(Fig. 6, page 3)***, add nostrils to front of Muzzle and add mouth below nostrils.

With Gold and Black embroidery floss, add open eyes ***(see Facial Features, page 4)***.

## TWISTED CORD

Cut 2 pieces of Metallic, each **3 times** longer than the desired finished length. Holding both pieces together, fasten one end to a stationary object **or** have another person hold it; twist until ***tight***. Fold in half and let it twist itself; knot both ends and cut the loops on the folded end.

## LAMB

**Finished Size:** Approximately 2¼" tall

### BODY

***Note #1:*** Work in BLO throughout ***(Fig. 2, page 2)***.

***Note #2:*** Every few rounds, stuff lightly.

**Rnd 1** (Right side)**:** With White ch 2, 6 sc in second ch from hook; do **not** join, place marker ***(see Markers, page 2)***: 6 sc.

***Note:*** Loop a short piece of yarn around any stitch to mark last round as **right** side.

**Rnd 2:** 2 Sc in each sc around: 12 sc.

**Rnds 3-7:** Sc in each sc around.

To **decrease** (uses next 2 sc), pull up a loop in BLO of next 2 sc, YO and draw through all 3 loops on hook.

**Rnd 8:** Decrease around: 6 sc.

**Rnd 9:** (Skip next sc, slip st in next sc) twice, leave remaining 2 sc unworked.

**Wool:** Ch 2, **turn**; working in free loops of Rnds 1-8 ***(Fig. 3b, page 2)***, slip st in next sc on Rnd 8, (ch 2, slip st in next sc) around; finish off.

### HEAD

***Note:*** Every few rounds, stuff lightly.

**Rnd 1** (Right side)**:** With Black ch 2, 6 sc in second ch from hook; do **not** join, place marker: 6 sc.

***Note:*** Mark last round as **right** side.

**Rnds 2 and 3:** Sc in each sc around, changing to White in last sc of Rnd 3 ***(Fig, 1, page 2)***.

**Rnd 4:** 2 Sc in each sc around: 12 sc.

***Note:*** Begin working in BLO.

***Rnds 5 and 6:*** Sc in each sc around.

**Rnd 7:** Decrease around: 6 sc.

**Rnd 8:** (Skip next sc, slip st in next sc) twice, leave remaining 2 sc unworked; finish off leaving a long end for sewing.

**Wool:** With **right** side facing, Rnd 1 of Head toward you, and working in free loops of Rnds 4-7, join White with slip st in first sc on Rnd 4; (ch 2, slip st in next sc) around; finish off.

### LEG (Make 4)

***Note:*** Every few rounds, stuff lightly.

**Rnd 1** (Right side)**:** With Black ch 2, 4 sc in second ch from hook; do **not** join, place marker: 4 sc.

**Note:** Mark last round as **right** side.

**Rnd 2**: Sc in each sc around, changing to White in last sc.

**Rnd 3:** (Sc in next sc, 2 sc in next sc) around: 6 sc.

***Note:*** Begin working in BLO.

**Rnds 4 and 5:** Sc in each sc around. Finish off, leaving a long end for sewing.

**Wool:** With **right** side facing, Rnd 1 of Leg toward you and working in free loops of Rnds 3 and 4, join White with slip st in first sc on Rnd 3; (ch 2, slip st in next sc) around; finish off.

### EAR (Make 2)

With Black, ch 4 **loosely**; sc in second ch from hook and in each ch across; finish off leaving a long end for sewing.

### TAIL

Work same as Ear.

### FINISHING

Using Cover Photo as a guide for placement, sew Head and Legs to Body; sew Ears to Head and Tail to back of Body.

With Blue embroidery floss and working Satin Stitch ***(Fig. 8, page 3)***, add eyes between Rnds 3 and 4 of Head.

## DONKEY

**Finished Size:** Approximately 7" tall

### HEAD

**Rnd 1** (Right side)***:*** With Light Peach ch 2, 6 sc in second ch from hook; do **not** join, place marker ***(see Markers, page 2)***: 6 sc.

***Note:*** Loop a short piece of yarn around any stitch to mark last round as **right** side.

**Rnd 2**: Sc in each sc around.

**Rnd 3:** (Sc in next sc, 2 sc in next sc) around, changing to Grey in last sc ***(Fig. 1, page 2)***: 9 sc.

**Rnds 4 and 5:** Sc in each sc around.

**Rnd 6:** (Sc in next 2 sc, 2 sc in next sc) around: 12 sc.

**Rnd 7:** (Sc in next 3 sc, 2 sc in next sc) around: 15 sc.

**Rnd 8:** (Sc in next 4 sc, 2 sc in next sc) around: 18 sc.

**Rnds 9 and 10:** Sc in each sc around.

Stuff lightly.

To **decrease** (uses next 2 sc), pull up a loop in next 2 sc, YO and draw through all 3 loops on hook.

**Rnd 11:** (Sc in next sc, decrease) around: 12 sc.

**Rnd 12:** Decrease around: 6 sc.

**Rnd 13:** (Skip next sc, slip st in next sc) around; finish off.

## BODY

**Note:** Every few rounds, stuff lightly.

**Rnd 1** (Right side)**:** With Grey ch 2, 6 sc in second ch from hook; do **not** join, place marker: 6 sc.

***Note:*** Mark last round as **right** side.

**Rnd 2**: 2 Sc in each sc around: 12 sc.

**Rnd 3:** (Sc in next sc, 2 sc in next sc) around: 18 sc.

**Rnds 4 and 5:** Sc in each sc around.

**Rnd 6:** (Sc in next 4 sc, decrease) around: 15 sc.

**Rnds 7-10:** Sc in each sc around.

**Rnd 11:** (Sc in next 4 sc, 2 sc in next sc) around: 18 sc.

**Rnds 12-14:** Sc in each sc around.

**Rnd 15:** (Sc in next sc, decrease) around: 12 sc.

**Rnd 16:** Decrease around: 6 sc.

**Rnd 17:** (Skip next sc, slip st in next sc) around; finish off.

## NECK

With Grey, ch 12 **loosely**; being careful not to twist ch, join with slip st to form a ring.

**Rnd 1** (Right side)**:** Ch 1, sc in each ch around; do **not** join, place marker: 12 sc.

***Note:*** Mark last round as **right** side.

**Rnd 2**: Sc in each sc around.

**Rnd 3:** (Sc in next 3 sc, 2 sc in next sc) around; 15 sc.

**Rnd 4:** Sc in each sc around, slip st in next sc; finish off leaving a long end for sewing.

## LEG (Make 4)

***Note:*** Every few rounds, stuff lightly.

**Rnd 1** (Right side)**:** With Black ch 2, 6 sc in second ch from hook, changing to Grey in last sc; do **not** join, place marker: 6 sc.

**Rnds 2-6:** Sc in each sc around.

**Rnd 7:** (Sc in next sc, 2 sc in next sc) around: 9 sc.

**Rnd 8:** Sc in each sc around.

**Rnd 9:** (Sc in next sc, decrease) around: 6 sc.

**Rnds 10-12:** Sc in each sc around.

**Rnd 13:** (Sc in next sc, 2 sc in next sc) around: 9 sc.

**Rnd 14:** (Sc in next 2 sc, 2 sc in next sc) around, slip st in next sc; finish off leaving a long end for sewing.

## EAR (Make 2)

With Grey, ch 7 **loosely**; sc in second ch from hook, hdc in next 4 chs, slip st in last ch; finish off leaving a long end for sewing.

## TAIL

With Grey, ch 11 **loosely;** slip st in second ch from hook and in each ch across; finish off leaving a long end for sewing.

## BLANKET

With Light Brown, ch 6 **loosely**.

**Row 1** (Right side)**:** Sc in second ch from hook and in each ch across: 5 sc.

***Note:*** Mark last row as **right** side.

**Row 2:** Ch 1, turn; sc in each sc across, changing to Dark Brown in last sc.

**Row 3:** Ch 1, turn; sc in first sc, ★ work long sc ***(Fig. 4, page 2)***, sc in next sc; repeat from ★ across.

**Row 4:** Ch 1, turn; sc in each sc across, changing to Light Brown in last sc.

**Row 5:** Ch 1, turn; sc in first sc, (work long sc, sc in next sc) across.

**Rows 6-13:** Repeat Rows 2-5 twice.

**Row 14:** Ch 1, turn; sc in each sc across; finish off. Add Fringe to each end ***(Figs. 9a & b, page 3)***.

## FINISHING

Using Cover Photo as a guide for placement, sew Rnd 4 of Neck to Body; stuff Neck lightly.
Sew Head to Neck with last round of Head facing toward back of Body.
Sew Legs to Body.
Sew Ears to Head and Tail to Body.
Place Blanket on back and sew in place.

Cut 2 strands of Dark Grey each 2" long. Hold together and tie in a knot onto end of Tail. Trim to ½".

★ Cut several 4" strands of Dark Grey; tie in center with a 10" strand to form a portion of Mane. Using long end, attach to Head. Trim to desired length and brush. Repeat from ★ to form entire Mane.

With Black and working Straight Stitch ***(Fig. 6, page 3)***, add nostrils.

With Light Peach and working Satin Stitch ***(Fig. 8, page 3)***, add eyes. With Black embroidery floss and working over center stitch, add pupil.

Show us what you're working on!

Share your project photos with us on social media.
Tag us @leisureartsinc or use #leisurearts

Items made and instructions tested by JoAnn Bowling, Pat Little, and Donna Soellner.

We have made every effort to ensure that these instructions are accurate and complete. We cannot, however, be responsible for human error, typographical mistakes, or variations in individual work.



Made in U.S.A.